UPLIFTING MEDITATIVE CALMING

MINDSSAGE

COLOURING BOOK

WORDS

MATTER

VOLUME 1

BY SOULA BERDOUSSIS - NEOFOTISTOS

MINDSSAGE COLOURING BOOK BELONGS TO

_____

ISBN: 978- 0- 9953362 - 1 - 6

Printed in the United States of America

Created and Published by Soula Neofotistos

First Edition - Volume 1

www.mindssagecolouringbooks.com

This series was created with the purpose of promoting effective communication and building self-esteem and confidence. All while people of all ages enjoy a wonderful, creative doodle and colouring pastime.

Imagine being inspired by beautifully chosen uplifting, meditative and calming positive words to colour. MINDSSAGE Colouring Book series provides just that! As an EFT Life Coach and Creator of the Mindssage Colouring Book series, I have combined my knowledge of the importance of the words you choose and the way you use them with a practice of mindfulness through colouring. The repetition of the positive and enlightening words on each colouring page is all you need to start to attract a more positive experience of life. And you will discover the creative colourist that you are.

It's a whole new colouring world with words
-There aren't any rules. You can colour inside the lines, outside the lines, in one colour or in dozens of colours.
-You can do candy cane-colouring, halfsies-colouring, and bubble gum-colouring (see website).

Benefits of Colouring

- memory improvement   - de stressing
- expressing yourself   - developing your focusing skills
- personal creativity - developing your mindfulness skills
- massaging and relaxing the mind

What is: "Doodle Dee and Doodle Lou" page?
Doodling is an extension of your imagination where
you allow your inner greatness to come to life on a
piece of paper.

Simply put, this is YOUR time and YOU decide what
to doodle and what to colour.

So... choose your favourite spot, grab your
MINDSSAGE Colouring Book, pick your favourite
colouring pencils, unplug all digital devices and start
the fun!

DOODLE DEE AND DOODLE LOU

LOVE
LOVE love
LOVE LOVE LOVE
LOVE LOVE
LOVE
LOVE
LOVE love
LOVE love
LOVE

LOVE... is at the root of all creation

DOODLE DEE AND DOODLE LOU

EXCITED

EXCITED

EXCITED

EXCITED

EXCITED

EXCITED

EXCITED

EXCITED

EXCITED

EXCITED

excited

EXCITED

EXCITED

EXCITED

EXCITED

EXCITED

EXCITED... the feeling from within

DOODLE DEE AND DOODLE LOU

HARMONY
HARMONY
HARMONY
HARMONY
HARMONY
HARMONY
HARMONY
HARMONY
HARMONY
harmony
HARMONY
HARMONY
HARMONY
HARMONY
HARMONY
harmony
HARMONY
HARMONY

HARMONY... uniting peacefully

DOODLE DEE AND DOODLE LOU

PEACEFUL
PEACEFUL
PEACEFUL
PEACEFUL
PEACEFUL
peaceful
Pea ceful
PEACEFUL
PEACEFUL
PEACEFUL
PEACEFUL
PEACEFUL
PEACEFUL
PEACEFUL
PEACEFUL
PEACEFUL

PEACEFUL... times of peace

DOODLE DEE AND DOODLE LOU

LIVING LIVING LIVING
LIVING LIVING LIVING
LIVING living LIVING
LIVING LIVING
LIVING LIVING
LIVING
living
LIVING

LIVING... a daily nourishment

DOODLE DEE AND DOODLE LOU

LIFE... life will always continue

DOODLE DEE AND DOODLE LOU

GROWTH... a magical process

DOODLE DEE AND DOODLE LOU

VISIONARY
VISIONARY
VISIONARY
VISIONARY
VISIONARY
VISIONARY
visionary
VISIONARY
VISIONARY
VISIONARY
visionary
VISIONARY
VISIONARY
VISIONARY
VISIONARY
VISIONARY
VISIONARY

VISIONARY... you see it now... what will be

DOODLE DEE AND DOODLE LOU

TRANSFORMATION
transformation
transformation
TRANSFORMATION
TRANSFORMATION
TRANSFORMATION
TRANSFORMATION
TRANSFORMATION
transformation
Transformation
TRANSFORMATION

TRANSFORMATION... be the change you would like to see

DOODLE DEE AND DOODLE LOU

EMPOWERMENT
EMPOWERMENT EMPOWERMENT
empowerment
empowerment empowerment
EMPOWERMENT
EMPOWERMENT
EMPOWERMENT
EMPOWERMENT
EMPOWERMENT
empowerment
EMPOWERMENT
EMPOWERMENT
EMPOWERMENT
EMPOWERMENT
EMPOWERMENT

EMPOWERMENT... understand the power is in you
and always has been - find it

DOODLE DEE AND DOODLE LOU

GRACE
grace
grace
GRACE
GRACE
GRACE
grace
GRACE
grace
GRACE
Grace
Grace
GRACE
GRACE
GRACE
GRACE
grace
GRACE
grace
GRACE

GRACE... stand up and be present

DOODLE DEE AND DOODLE LOU

ACCEPT... recognize and be aware of what is true

DOODLE DEE AND DOODLE LOU

FUN FUN FUN FUN FUN
FUN FUN FUN FUN FUN
FUN FUN FUN FUN FUN
FUN FUN FUN FUN FUN
FUN FUN FUN FUN FUN
FUN FUN FUN FUN FUN
FUN FUN FUN FUN FUN

FUN... look around... the amusement can be
heard and felt everywhere

DOODLE DEE AND DOODLE LOU

SIMPLE SIMPLE SIMPLE
SIMPLE SIMPLE SIMPLE
SIMPLE simple SIMPLE
SIMPLE SIMPLE SIMPLE
SIMPLE SIMPLE
SIMPLE simple
SIMPLE SIMPLE

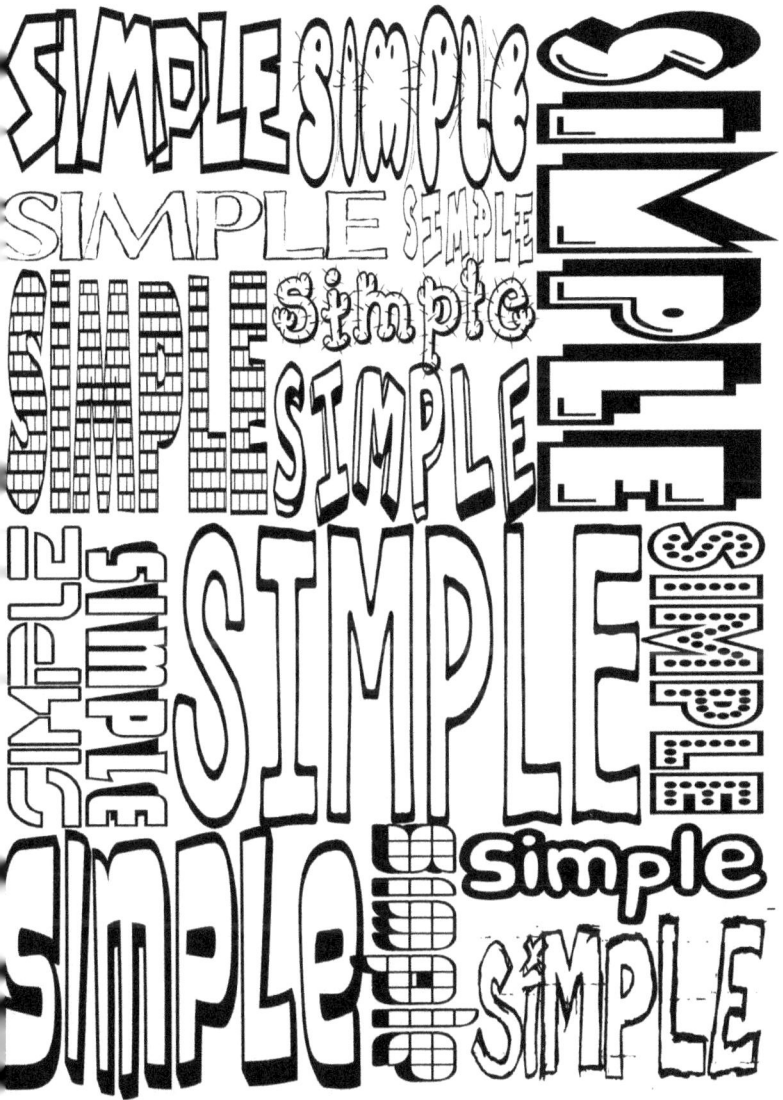

SIMPLE... easily understood with no difficulty

DOODLE DEE AND DOODLE LOU

MINDFULNESS
MINDFULNESS
MINDFULNESS
MINDFULNESS
MINDFULNESS
MINDFULNESS
MINDFULNESS
MINDFULNESS
MINDFULNESS
mindfulness
mindfulness
MINDFULNESS
MINDFULNESS
MINDFULNESS
mindfulness
mindfulness
MINDFULNESS
MINDFULNESS
MINDFULNESS
mindfulness
mindfulness

MIDNFULNESS... try living in the "NOW"

DOODLE DEE AND DOODLE LOU

Laughter
LAUGHTER
LAUGHTER
LAUGHTER
LAUGHTER
LAUGHTER
laughter LAUGHTER
LAUGHTER
LAUGHTER
laughter LAUGHTER
LAUGHTER LAUGHTER
LAUGHTER

LAUGHTER... sound of amusement coming
from the heart

DOODLE DEE AND DOODLE LOU

THINK THINK THINK
THINK THINK THINK
THINK THINK
THINK
THINK THINK
THINK
THINK
THINK THINK THINK THINK THINK
THINK think think THINK THINK

THINK... think about it for a minute...
think... think.... think!

DOODLE DEE AND DOODLE LOU

HAPPY HAPPY HAPPY HAPPY
HAPPY HAPPY HAPPY HAPPY
HAPPY HAPPY HAPPY HAPPY
happy HAPPY
HAPPY HAPPY HAPPY
HAPPY HAPPY HAPPY HAPPY HAPPY
HAPPY HAPPY

HAPPY... a pleasure to be around

DOODLE DEE AND DOODLE LOU

FREEDOM
FREEDOM
FREEDOM
FREEDOM
FREEDOM
FREEDOM
FREEDOM
FREEDOM
FREEDOM
freedom
FREEDOM
FREEDOM
FREEDOM
FREEDOM
FREEDOM
FREEDOM
FREEDOM
FREEDOM
FREEDOM
FREEDOM

FREEDOM... flying like a bird

DOODLE DEE AND DOODLE LOU

FOCUS... where your interests are

DOODLE DEE AND DOODLE LOU

clarity CLARITY
clarity CLARITY
CLARITY CLARITY CLARITY
CLARITY CLARITY
CLARITY
CLARITY
CLARITY
CLARITY CLARITY
CLARITY
CLARITY

CLARITY... particularly clear about what I am doing

DOODLE DEE AND DOODLE LOU

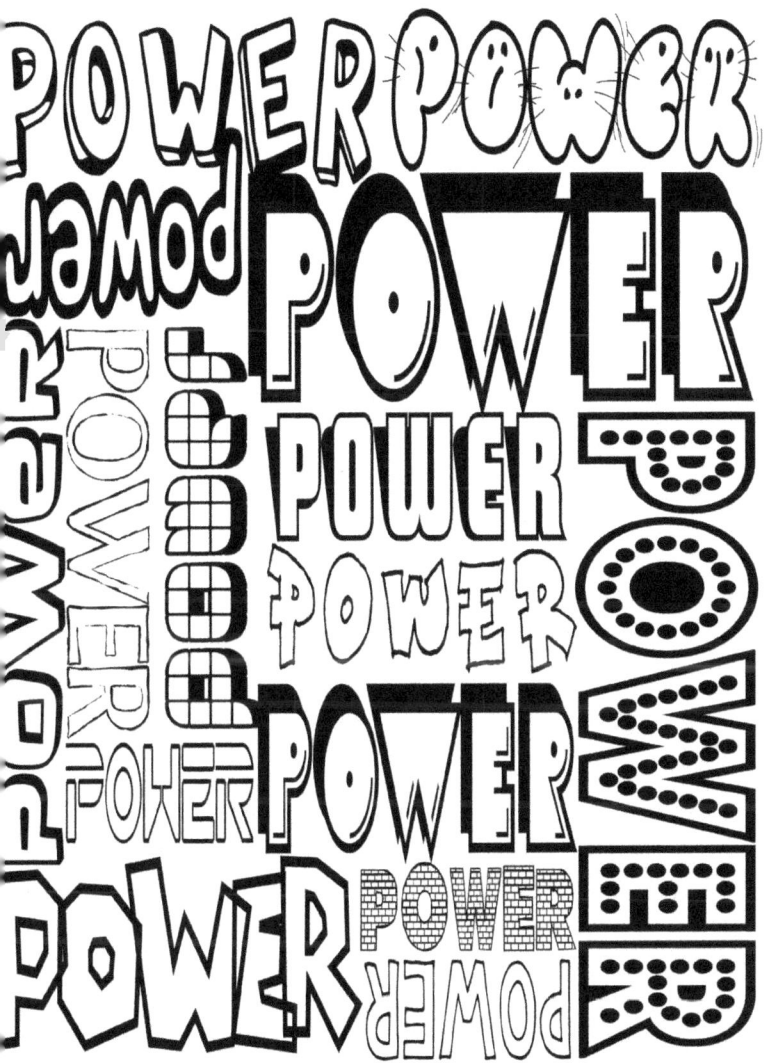

POWER... direct or influence in the right way

DOODLE DEE AND DOODLE LOU

BLISS... reaching a state of perfect happiness

DOODLE DEE AND DOODLE LOU

FORGIVE
FORGIVE
FORGIVE
FORGIVE
forgive
FORGIVE
FORGIVE
FORGIVE
FORGIVE
FORGIVE
FORGIVE
FORGIVE
FORGIVE
FORGIVE
FORGIVE
FORGIVE
FORGIVE
FORGIVE
FORGIVE
FORGIVE

FORGIVE... set yourself free

DOODLE DEE AND DOODLE LOU

DREAM DREAM DREAM
DREAM DREAM DREAM
DREAM DREAM DREAM
DREAM DREAM DREAM
DREAM DREAM DREAM
DREAM DREAM DREAM
DREAM DREAM DREAM

DREAM... floating thoughts, images, and emotions

DOODLE DEE AND DOODLE LOU

PLAYING
PLAYING
playing
PLAYING
PLAYING
PLAYING
PLAYING
PLAYING
PLAYING
PLAYING
PLAYING
PLAYING
PLAYING
PLAYING
playing
PLAYING
PLAYING
playing
PLAYING
PLAYING

PLAYING... take part

DOODLE DEE AND DOODLE LOU

DECIDE
DECIDE
DECIDE
DECIDE
DECIDE
DECIDE
DECIDE
DECIDE
DECIDE
DECIDE
DECIDE
decide
DECIDE
DECIDE
DECIDE
decide

DECIDE... make up your mind

DOODLE DEE AND DOODLE LOU

LEADER
LEADER
LEADER
LEADER
LEADER
Leader
LEADER
leader
LEADER
LEADER
LEADER
LEADER
LEADER
LEADER
LEADER
LEADER
LEADER

LEADER... builder of sorts

DOODLE DEE AND DOODLE LOU

AMBITIOUS
AMBITIOUS
AMBITIOUS
AMBITIOUS
AMBITIOUS
AMBITIOUS
AMBITIOUS
AMBITIOUS
AMBITIOUS
AMBITIOUS
ambitious
AMBITIOUS
AMBITIOUS
ambitious
AMBITIOUS

AMBITIOUS... live the dream

DOODLE DEE AND DOODLE LOU

SUNSHINE
SUNSHINE
SUNSHINE
SUNSHINE
SUNSHINE
SUNSHINE
SUNSHINE
SUNSHINE
SUNSHINE
SUNSHINE
sunshine
SUNSHINE
SUNSHINE
SUNSHINE
SUNSHINE
SUNSHINE

SUNSHINE... brightens the world

DOODLE DEE AND DOODLE LOU

EFFECTIVE

effective

EFFECTIVE

EFFECTIVE

EFFECTIVE

EFFECTIVE

EFFECTIVE

EFFECTIVE

EFFECTIVE

EFFECTIVE

EFFECTIVE

EFFECTIVE... see yourself putting
one foot in front of the other

DOODLE DEE AND DOODLE LOU

MEDITATION
MEDITATION
MEDITATION
MEDITATION
MEDITATION
MEDITATION
MEDITATION
MEDITATION
MEDITATION
MEDITATION
MEDITATION
MEDITATION
MEDITATION
MEDITATION
MEDITATION
MEDITATION
MEDITATION
MEDITATION

MEDITATION... preparing to clear things out

DOODLE DEE AND DOODLE LOU

HEALING HEALING HEALING

HEALING HEALING HEALING

HEALING Healing HEALING

HEALING HEALING

healing HEALING HEALING

HEALING HEALING

HEALING... everything is new and wonderful

DOODLE DEE AND DOODLE LOU

ENCOURAGE
ENCOURAGE
ENCOURAGE
ENCOURAGE
ENCOURAGE
encourage
ENCOURAGE
ENCOURAGE
ENCOURAGE
ENCOURAGE
ENCOURAGE
ENCOURAGE
encourage

ENCOURAGE... sparkle and grow

DOODLE DEE AND DOODLE LOU

JOY JOY JOY JOY JOY JOY JOY JOY JOY JOY JOY JOY JOY JOY JOY JOY JOY JOY JOY JOY JOY JOY JOY JOY JOY JOY JOY JOY JOY

JOY... the feeling of getting
what you always wanted

DOODLE DEE AND DOODLE LOU

INSPIRE
INSPIRE
INSPIRE
INSPIRE
INSPIRE
INSPIRE
INSPIRE
INSPIRE
INSPIRE
INSPIRE
INSPIRE
inspire
INSPIRE
inspire
INSPIRE
INSPIRE
INSPIRE INSPIRE

INSPIRE... filling up with vision

DOODLE DEE AND DOODLE LOU

TERRIFIC
TERRIFIC
TERRIFIC
TERRIFIC
TERRIFIC
TERRIFIC
TERRIFIC
TERRIFIC
TERRIFIC
TERRIFIC
TERRIFIC
terrific
TERRIFIC
TERRIFIC
TERRIFIC
TERRIFIC

TERRIFIC... awesome... great... good

DOODLE DEE AND DOODLE LOU

SPECIAL SPECIAL SPECIAL SPECIAL SPECIAL

SPECIAL SPECIAL SPECIAL SPECIAL

SPECIAL SPECIAL SPECIAL

SPECIAL

SPECIAL SPECIAL

SPECIAL SPECIAL Special SPECIAL

SPECIAL... different than the usual

DOODLE DEE AND DOODLE LOU

CREATE
CREATE
CREATE
CREATE
CREATE
CREATE
CREATE
CREATE
CREATE
CREATE
CREATE
CREATE
CREATE
CREATE
CREATE
CREATE
CREATE
CREATE
create
CREATE

CREATE... sowing the seeds

DOODLE DEE AND DOODLE LOU

ENGAGE
ENGAGE
ENGAGE
ENGAGE
engage
ENGAGE
ENGAGE
ENGAGE
ENGAGE
ENGAGE
ENGAGE
ENGAGE
ENGAGE
ENGAGE
ENGAGE
ENGAGE
ENGAGE
engage

ENGAGE... getting involved is so much fun

DOODLE DEE AND DOODLE LOU

ABUNDANCE
ABUNDANCE
ABUNDANCE
ABUNDANCE
ABUNDANCE
ABUNDANCE
ABUNDANCE
ABUNDANCE
ABUNDANCE
ABUNDANCE
ABUNDANCE
ABUNDANCE
ABUNDANCE
ABUNDANCE
ABUNDANCE
ABUNDANCE
abundance
ABUNDANCE
ABUNDANCE
ABUNDANCE

ABUNDANCE... overflowing and keep it coming

DOODLE DEE AND DOODLE LOU

THANKFUL
THANKFUL
THANKFUL
THANKFUL
THANKFUL
THANKFUL
THANKFUL
THANKFUL
THANKFUL
thankful
THANKFUL
THANKFUL
THANKFUL
THANKFUL

THANKFUL... it all worked out just like I thought

DOODLE DEE AND DOODLE LOU

JOLLY
JOLLY
JOLLY
JOLLY
JOLLY
JOLLY
JOLLY
JOLLY
JOLLY
JOLLY
JOLLY
JOLLY
JOLLY
JOLLY
JOLLY
JOLLY
JOLLY
JOLLY
JOLLY
JOLLY

JOLLY... full abundance of cheer

DOODLE DEE AND DOODLE LOU

OPTIMISTIC
OPTIMISTIC
optimistic
OPTIMISTIC
OPTIMISTIC
OPTIMISTIC
OPTIMISTIC
OPTIMISTIC
OPTIMISTIC
OPTIMISTIC
OPTIMISTIC
OPTIMISTIC
OPTIMISTIC
OPTIMISTIC
OPTIMISTIC... future is looking pretty good

DOODLE DEE AND DOODLE LOU

delightful

DELIGHTFUL

DELIGHTFUL

DELIGHTFUL

DELIGHTFUL

DELIGHTFUL

DELIGHTFUL

DELIGHTFUL

DELIGHTFUL

DELIGHTFUL

DELIGHTFUL

DELIGHTFUL

DELIGHTFUL

DELIGHTFUL

DELIGHTFUL... pleasantly pleasant

DOODLE DEE AND DOODLE LOU

ENERGY
ENERGY
ENERGY
ENERGY
ENERGY
ENERGY
ENERGY
ENERGY
ENERGY
ENERGY
ENERGY
ENERGY
ENERGY
ENERGY
ENERGY

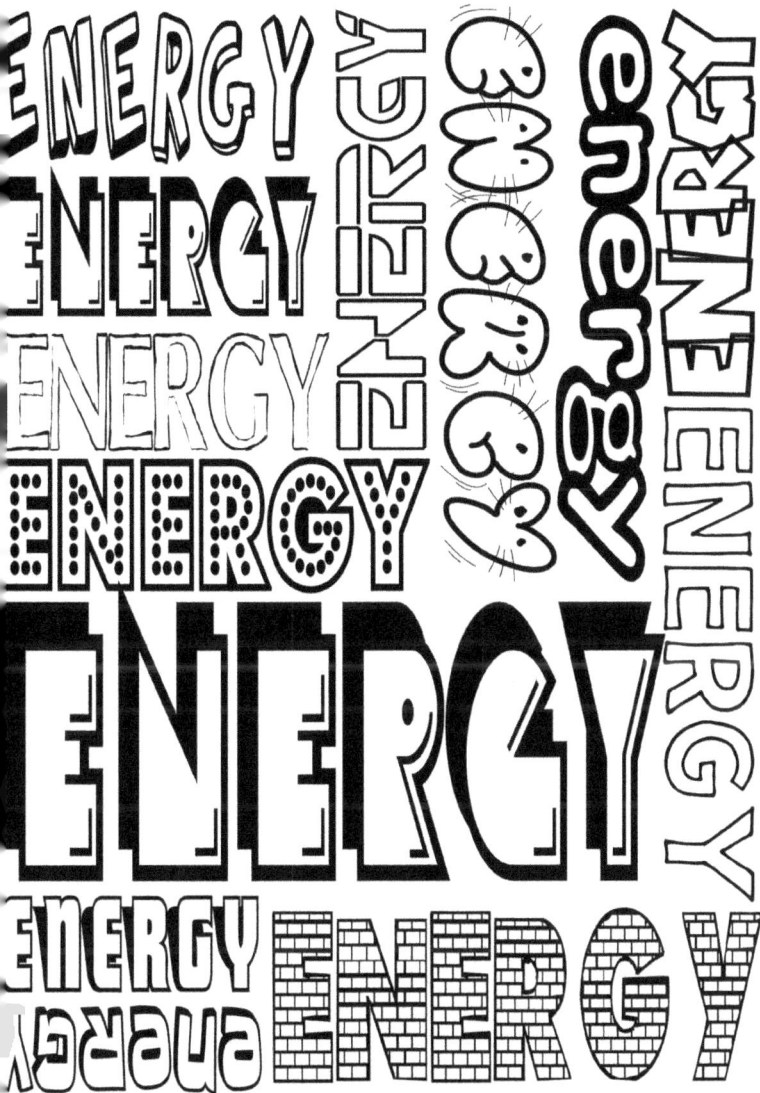

ENERGY... the power source for all

DOODLE DEE AND DOODLE LOU

SMILE SMILE smile SMILE SMILE SMILE
SMILE SMILE SMILE SMILE
SMILE SMILE SMILE
SMILE SMILE
SMILE SMILE SMILE
SMILE SMILE
SMILE SMILE

SMILE... brightens up the face

DOODLE DEE AND DOODLE LOU

IMAGINE
IMAGINE
imagine
IMAGINE
IMAGINE
IMAGINE
IMAGINE
IMAGINE
IMAGINE
IMAGINE
IMAGINE

IMAGINE

imagine
imagine
IMAGINE
IMAGINE
imagine
IMAGINE
IMAGINE
IMAGINE

IMAGINE... seeing is believing

DOODLE DEE AND DOODLE LOU

TITLES AVAILABLE

WORDS MATTER

I AM MATTERS

CONFIDENCE MATTERS

INSPIRATION MATTERS

COMING SOON

WORDS MATTER II

BIBLE WORDS MATTER

THINKING MATTERS

REMEMBER A GOOD TIME MATTERS

TAKING A BREAK MATTERS

ASKING YOURSELF MATTERS

ASKING YOURSELF MATTERS II